Central Park

THEN AND NOW

Central Park

THEN AND NOW

Marcia Reiss

THUNDER BAY
P·R·E·S·S

San Diego, California

Thunder Bay Press
An imprint of the Baker & Taylor Publishing Group
10350 Barnes Canyon Road, San Diego, CA 92121
www.thunderbaybooks.com

Produced by Salamander Books, an imprint of Anova Books Ltd.
10 Southcombe Street, London W14 0RA, UK

"Then and Now" is a registered trademark of Anova Books Ltd.

Library of Congress Cataloging-in-Publication Data

Reiss, Marcia.
  Central Park then & now / Marcia Reiss.
    p. cm.
  ISBN-13: 978-1-60710-007-2
  ISBN-10: 1-60710-007-X
  1. Central Park (New York, N.Y.)--Pictorial works. 2. Central Park (New York, N.Y.)--
History--Pictorial works. 3. New York (N.Y.)--Pictorial works. 4. New York (N.Y.)--
History--Pictorial works. 5. Repeat photography--New York (State)--New York.
I. Title. II. Title: Central Park then and now.
  F128.65.C3R45 2010
  974.7'1--dc22
                                              2009037304

1 2 3 4 5 14 13 12 11 10

Printed in China

To my friend and colleague Linda Davidoff (1941–2003), an inspirational advocate for public parks.

Acknowledgments

Thanks first, as always, to my husband Charles Reiss for his unwavering support and uncanny ability to
pinpoint the background buildings in historic New York scenes. Also to Frank Margeson for his creative
photography and determination to find the perfect contemporary match for the archival images. And to
Jerilyn Perine and Christopher Gray for their kind and patient assistance in helping me identify particularly
puzzling archival scenes. Thanks also to Sara Cedar Miller, Central Park's historian and photographer, for
her knowledgeable assistance.

The author drew on the following publications for information:

Elizabeth Blackmar and Roy Rosenzweig, *The Park and the People*, Cornell University Press,
    Ithaca and London, 1992.
Raymond Carroll, *Complete Illustrated Map and Guidebook to Central Park*, Barnes and Noble,
    Silver Lining Books, New York, 2001.
Morrison H. Heckscher, *Creating Central Park*, Metropolitan Museum of Art, 2008.
Sara Cedar Miller, *Central Park, An American Masterpiece*, Abrams, New York, 2003.
Henry Hope Reed, Robert McGee and Esther Mippas, *Bridges of Central Park*,
    Greensward Foundation, Inc., New York, 1990.
Kate Simon, *Fifth Avenue: A Very Social History*, Harcourt Brace Jovanovich, New York, 1978.
Robert A.M. Stern, et al. *New York 1880; New York 1900; New York 1930; New York 1960;
    New York 2000*, Monacelli Press and Rizzoli, New York.

Picture Credits

"Then" photographs: **Corbis:** 142; 6, 20, 22 main, 24, 34 main, 38, 46, 48 main, 62 inset, 64, 66, 74, 76 inset,
82, 96, 100, 102, 108, 116, 120, 122, 128, 134, 140 (Bettmann/Corbis); 14 (Underwood & Underwood/Corbis);
36 (Roger Wood/Corbis); 76 main, 138 (Photo Collection Alexander Alland, Sr./Corbis); 86 (Lebrecht Music &
Arts/Corbis). **Getty Images:** 70 main, 112. **Library of Congress:** 8 (LC-D4-36551), 12 main (LC-D4-43752), 12
inset (LC-USW3-007824-E), 16 (LC-B2-1419-14), 22 inset (LC-USZ62-100547), 30 (LC-G612-T01-17859), 32
(LC-USZ62-119536), 34 inset (LC-DIG-ggbain-08146), 42 (LC-D4-12685), 44–45 (LC-USZ62-121334), 48 inset
(LC-DIG-ggbain-08167), 50 (LC-USW3-007857-E), 52 (LC-USZ62-69575), 54–55 (LC-USZ62-121333), 56 (LC-
USW3-007792-E), 60 main (LC-USZ62-11356), 60 inset (LC-D4-13306), 62 main (LC-USZ62-94238), 70 inset
(LC-USZ62-52253), 72 main (LC-USZ62-101736), 72 inset (LC-D401-13093), 78 main (LC-DIG-ggbain-35882),
78 inset (LC-USZ62-57467), 80 (HAER NY,31-NEYO,153C-2), 90 (LC-USZ62-74032), 92 (LC-G612-T01-18254),
98 (HAER NY,31-NEYO,153F-1), 104 (LC-DIG-ggbain-20618), 106 (LC-D4-33887), 110 (LC-USZ62-52269), 114
(LC-G612-T-45559), 118 main (LC-DIG-ggbain-10404), 118 inset (LC-DIG-ggbain-10405), 126 (LC-DIG-ggbain-
21394), 130 (LC-USZ62-100272), 132 (LC-DIG-ggbain-13035). **Museum of the City of New York:** 40. **New York
City Department of Parks & Recreation:** 84. **New York Public Library:** 10, 18, 26, 58, 68, 88, 94, 124, 136.

"Now" photographs: All "Now" images were taken by Frank Margeson, except for pages 7 (David
Ball/Corbis); 39 (Denise Stephens); 57 main (John Blough); 59 (Robert Catalano); 119 (Corbis); 141
(Rob Howard/Corbis); 143 (Evan Joseph; http://www.evanjoseph.com/).

Pages 1 and 3 show Wollman Rink, then (Bettmann/Corbis) and now (Frank Margeson). Endpapers show
imagined renderings of Central Park before it was completed (Museum of the City of New York/Corbis). On
the left is an 1865 view looking south from the lake toward Bethesda Terrace and the tree-lined Mall. On
the right is an 1863 bird's-eye view of the entire park looking north. The map on page 144 is courtesy of Central
Park Conservancy.

Introduction

Central Park is perhaps the best-known park in America, instantly recognizable as a New York City icon. Although the park is virtually synonymous with New York, every feature—its vast open space, bucolic scenery, quaint structures, and lush landscape—is a dramatic contrast to the city itself. Visitors to the park are often surprised to discover that this city of concrete and steel—the most densely populated metropolis in the nation—has an enormous green heart.

Even more surprising is the fact that, like the city, Central Park is completely man-made. Its romantic design of rolling meadows, dense woodlands, and serene water bodies was a feat of engineering, requiring the latest technology of the day.

It is the creation of two gifted designers, Frederick Law Olmsted (1822–1903), a journalist with no training or experience other than surveying and farming, and Calvert Vaux (1824–95), a British architect with a talent for landscape art. Together, they won the design competition for the park in 1858 and over the next fifteen years—through the seemingly insurmountable obstacles of the Civil War, financial crises, and municipal corruption—transformed a wasteland into a public Eden.

The site included 843 acres of swampy and rocky land—much of it an unofficial dumping ground—at the northern reaches of Manhattan. Olmsted supervised thousands of men, at times as many as 4,000 at once, to move nearly five million cubic yards of stone, earth, and topsoil. They reshaped the terrain, laid miles of drainage tiles, and built a complex system of bridges, arches, and overpasses above sunken transverse roads. Vaux designed most of the park structures, including the graceful bridges and exquisite buildings. After the first two years of construction, the public was able to ice-skate and boat on a newly formed lake, ride carriages on landscaped drives, and hike through an artfully created forest known as the Ramble. Largely completed in 1873, the park was one of the greatest public works of the nineteenth century, an achievement as magnificent as the construction of the Brooklyn Bridge.

Modeled after English country parks, it was also uniquely inspired by the democratic vision of a "pleasure ground for all classes." Newspaper publisher William Cullen Bryant began the campaign for a major park in New York City in 1844 as a much-needed place for the city's poor, who could not find relief in countryside retreats. At the time, the city had only two public parks, both quite small. The city's elite also wanted a large park as a matter of civic pride, worthy of competition with European capitals, and as a "civilizing" environment for the working classes and the increasing number of immigrants.

Influential landowners and speculators also clearly recognized that adjacent real-estate values would soar. Indeed, after the park was completed, Upper Fifth Avenue was firmly established as "Millionaires' Row" where prominent families like the Vanderbilts and Astors lived in châteaulike mansions like feudal French lords. The tract of land set aside for the park was undeveloped but not uninhabited. Its construction displaced some 1,600 people who had lived there, both squatters and several hundred African American property owners in an established village.

As the park grew, so did the city. Maintaining the park has been as challenging as creating it. Throughout its history, it has faced repeated threats of decline and destruction. Olmsted, overworked and suffering from bouts of depression, was fired and resigned, but returned several times in the course of aesthetic, political, and financial battles with the corrupt city administration led by William "Boss" Tweed (1863–72). Later administrations allowed the park to deteriorate, and by the end of the 1920s it was seriously dilapidated and facing encroachment by proposals ranging from housing developments to an airport. Ironically, it was saved by the Great Depression when the forceful new city parks commissioner, Robert Moses, who served from 1934 to 1960, secured federal funds and became nearly as influential as Olmsted and Vaux had been in shaping the park. While Moses sacrificed some of the park's romantic landscape, he rescued it from disrepair, built a new zoo, added playgrounds, and instituted a system for proper maintenance.

Serious problems emerged again in the city's financial crisis of the 1970s when the park was overrun with dead grass, broken lampposts, crumbling walls, and graffiti-covered monuments. It was reborn in the 1980s with the formation of the Central Park Conservancy. The CPC conducted major campaigns to raise private funds and, to date, has invested more than $500 million in restoring the park—more than twice the original cost to build it, even in today's dollars. Today, its splendid features—the magnificent Mall, Terrace, Bethesda Fountain, and bridges—are as beautiful as they were in Olmsted and Vaux's time, perhaps even more so against the backdrop of the New York skyline. Even in dire times, the park has been immensely popular. In 1860, just two years after the start of construction, two and a half million visits to the park were recorded, three times more than Manhattan's population at the time. As the city grew, its population—ethnically, culturally, and economically diverse—made increasing, often conflicting demands on the park. From the start, debates raged over how or if the park should accommodate different activities. It was emerging in the 1860s just as the newly popular sport of baseball was taking hold and the debate about peaceful meadows vs. baseball diamonds continued throughout the nineteenth and twentieth centuries. It was also the subject of religious and cultural controversies, ranging from nineteenth-century rules against band concerts on Sundays to twentieth-century limits on rock concerts.

As the gathering place for major events, it has been a focal point for political and cultural change, from World War II victory rallies to mass protests against the Vietnam War. Huge crowds also have come to the park to protest the nuclear arms race, to celebrate Earth Day, to demonstrate for gay rights, and to see and hear the most popular musicians of the day, from Pavarotti to Simon and Garfunkel. It has been the setting for hundreds of films and countless publicity shots for visiting celebrities. Twenty-five million people now visit the park each year, more than any other urban park in the nation. Filled with people from every walk of life, Central Park has been, and still is, a microcosm of the city and an integral part of New York life.

CENTRAL PARK FROM THE AIR

Central Park was a force for development and a hedge against it

Left: This 1950 bird's-eye view leaves no doubt that without Central Park the city's relentless growth would have covered every inch of Manhattan. When park construction began in the 1860s, few buildings had risen above Fifty-ninth Street, seen here in the foreground. But park views were irresistible to real-estate developers. By the 1920s, skyscrapers were pushing hard against nearly every park border. Fortunately, by the mid-twentieth century, only one large building had penetrated the park, the Metropolitan Museum of Art, seen in the upper right background. The only other visible building is one that predated the park, the Arsenal, seen in the park's lower right corner.

Above: Today's view of the park surrounded by the city makes it clear that Central Park was both a force for development and a hedge against it. In a symbiotic process, the buildings hardened the park's edge, while the park's green expanse softened the effect of concrete and steel. The result is one of the most dramatic landscapes of any city in the world, an amazing contrast of urban density and pastoral beauty. Although a new mountain range of towers at the Fifty-ninth Street border blocks views of many familiar buildings, such as the Plaza Hotel (archival photo, right foreground), the park has held its ground, preserving rare commodities in New York: light, air, and space. The largest body of water in both photos is the Central Park Reservoir—renamed the Jacqueline Kennedy Onassis Reservoir in 1994. Built along with the park in the 1860s, this 106-acre basin, one of two reservoirs once located in the park, was once a major facility for city drinking water.

MILLIONAIRES' ROW

The park pulled millionaires up Fifth Avenue

Left: Central Park was a magnet for New York's wealthiest families. Lower Fifth Avenue had long been the best address, but once the park was completed in the 1870s, it pulled millionaires up the avenue. The châteaulike mansion on the left was built for Cornelius Vanderbilt II in 1879–82. Located between Fifty-seventh and Fifty-eighth streets, just a block below the Fifth Avenue entrance to the park, it occupied a prestigious site with unobstructed views of the park. Its trees are visible in the far background. Towering behind the mansion on the left is the Plaza Hotel (1907), whose opulent rooms also attracted a high-society crowd. Across the avenue from the Vanderbilt mansion is Marble Row, built in 1869 by Mary Mason Jones, Edith Wharton's aunt, who set the fashion for living near the park. Jones, the model for a character in Wharton's novel *The Age of Innocence*, was also the inspiration for the phrase, "keeping up with the Joneses."

Above: The Vanderbilt mansion was demolished in 1926 and Marble Row came down soon after, opening Fifth Avenue to commercial development. Cornelius Vanderbilt's widow sold the property so that she could stop paying $130,000 a year in taxes on her immense home. Its replacement was a large but elegant women's clothing store. Built in 1928 with a green mansard roof and white marble cladding, Bergdorf-Goodman's (center, left) looked like a French Renaissance palace. The business had prospered ever since Edwin Goodman, a tailor, teamed up with Herman Bergdorf in 1901. Goodman moved into an apartment on the top floor of the new building, fine quarters for a merchant who lived above the store. Today, Bergdorf's is a prestigious landmark all its own, a place where multimillionaires shop. The glass-walled building on the right is part of the luxurious shopping center in the Trump Tower (1983).

PULITZER FOUNTAIN

Newspaper publisher Joseph Pulitzer provided $50,000 for the fountain in his will

Left: Dedicated in 1916 at the southeastern corner of the park, the fountain was a gift from the estate of newspaper publisher Joseph Pulitzer. It is crowned by a statue of Pomona, goddess of abundance, an appropriate symbol for this location in front of the Vanderbilt mansion. Before Pulitzer died in 1911, he knew that his longtime publishing rival, William Randolph Hearst, was planning to sponsor a monument at the southwestern corner of the park. Hearst's monument was erected there in 1913 (see page 135). Pulitzer provided $50,000 for the fountain in his will and also got the last word with another combatant, General William T. Sherman, whose statue was already in place across from the fountain site (see page 12). Sherman hated the press, yet his statue faces the memorial to one of the most powerful newspapermen of his day.

Above: Cushioned by an arch of flowering trees, the graceful fountain softens the park's southern edge along its dense urban borders. Like most of the monuments in the park, it had deteriorated during the city's financial crisis of the 1970s. It lost its flanking columns and surrounding balustrades and suffered the final insult in 1980 when the water was turned off. With donations from adjacent building owners for plumbing and paving repairs, the water came back on in 1990. To pedestrians walking north to the park along Fifth Avenue, the fountain with its splashing water, new lighting, trees, and flower beds announces the beginning of a greener landscape and provides a welcome respite from tall buildings and traffic. Pulitzer's name is well known today for prestigious awards to journalists, writers, and composers.

GENERAL SHERMAN MONUMENT

A majestic presence at the park's Fifth Avenue entrance

Left: Ever since its installation in 1903, the statue of Civil War general William Tecumseh Sherman provided a majestic presence at the park's Fifth Avenue entrance. It is the last work of the great nineteenth-century sculptor Augustus Saint-Gaudens, who spent eleven years creating it through periods of serious illness. Sherman is famous for blazing the trail of destruction through Atlanta that led to the Confederacy's surrender. The female figure is a portrayal of Nike, Greek goddess of victory. While she carries a symbolic branch of peace, Sherman's horse tramples a branch of Georgia pine. The inset view was taken in 1942 when Americans were engaged in another great war.

Above: Saint-Gaudens gilded the statue with layers of gold leaf because he didn't want it to look like "a smokestack." Nevertheless, it was covered with city soot over the years and few New Yorkers remembered its original veneer. When it was restored in 1989 with bright gold, some critics felt the result was tacky. Time has weathered the shine and the criticism. Along with his scorched-earth treatment of Atlanta, Sherman is famous for saying "War is hell." Despite its bellicose history, the statue is a comfortable gathering place today.

PLAZA HOTEL

Designated a city landmark in 1969

Left: By the turn of the century, this site at the Fifth Avenue and Fifty-ninth Street entrance to Central Park was the preeminent place for a luxury hotel. The first Plaza Hotel, a classical structure by the architectural firm of McKim, Mead, and White, was built here in 1893. But it was considered outdated by 1905, and plans for the new hotel were laid by Henry Hardenbergh, architect of the first Waldorf-Astoria on Fifth Avenue and Thirty-fourth Street. The new Plaza Hotel, built in 1907 and seen here in the 1920s, soon eclipsed the Waldorf-Astoria as the most fashionable hotel of the day. It was here that American tycoons could follow the English lifestyle of living in country estates and spending the fashionable winter season in an elegant hotel. Goulds and Guggenheims lived in suites at the new Plaza, rubbing shoulders with visiting monarchs in the gilded dining rooms.

Above: Recognized as a crown jewel at the head of Central Park, the Plaza Hotel was designated a city landmark in 1969. While this prevented demolition, a series of hotel owners had already altered the fabled interior rooms, losing such splendid features as the Palm Court's Tiffany glass ceiling in 1943. By the late 1980s, the hotel's crown was noticeably tarnished. More owners—including Donald Trump, who refurbished the public rooms—came and left. In 2007, the year of its centennial, a new group of developers reopened the hotel with multimillion-dollar apartments. Strongly criticized for changing a New York tradition, they kept more than half of the rooms as hotel units—and re-created the lost glass ceiling. Although larger buildings loom alongside it, the Plaza Hotel still stands out as the most distinctive building along Central Park.

CARRIAGE DRIVE

Central Park gave wealthy New Yorkers a suitable place for carriage driving

To wealthy New Yorkers, one of the strongest arguments for building Central Park was to have a suitable place for carriage driving. For those who could afford carriages, a large park was a beautiful place to show them off, away from the noise, dirt, and all-too-common companionship of commercial traffic. Commercial wagons were banned from the park drives, restricted to the transverse roads that ran beneath the park. The drives were curved rather than straight to prevent racing by "fast trotters." Frederick Law Olmsted knew the perils of carriage riding from an accident in 1860 that left him with a pronounced limp for the rest of his life. Interestingly, the driver in this Victorian-era photo is a woman.

Ever since cars replaced horse-drawn vehicles, the only carriages in the park have been ones for hire. They gather on Central Park South waiting for customers, and the long line of horses on the street filled with cars and buses is a daily anachronism. A carriage ride through the park, portrayed in many movies, is considered a romantic and essential New York experience. But not everyone agrees. The Manhattan-based Coalition to Ban Horse-Drawn Carriages has long criticized the conditions that city horses must endure, particularly in the heat of summer when the animals risk overheating on hot asphalt. But once inside the park, both man and beast enjoy a welcome break from city traffic.

INSCOPE ARCH

One of the last arches to be built in the park

Above: Nearly forty bridges and arches were built in the park, each one a unique design. As practical as they are beautiful, they solved complex traffic problems presented by an intersecting system of three roads: carriage drives, pedestrian pathways, and bridle paths. This arch, located near East Sixty-second Street, relieved a bottleneck of traffic by passing under the heavily used East Drive. Built in 1875, it was one of the last arches to be built and was designed by Olmsted and Vaux's landscape architecture firm, which they formed after ending their official employment by the park in 1873.

Right: Today, the unusually wide structure, a beautiful combination of pink and gray granite, is just the way Olmsted and Vaux envisioned it, as an integral part of the sylvan setting. Like many of the arches in the park, it is on a curving pathway and comes as a pleasant surprise to pedestrians, in this case as they turn a corner between the Pond and Zoo. Its deep interior is a cool break from the summer sun and muffles the noise of cars on the drive above.

THE POND

Originally a swamp, the man-made Pond was artfully shaped into a naturalistic form

Left: Except for the unmistakably urban buildings in the background, this could be a scene in the country. But it began as something quite different. Before the park was built, this was Pigtown, a squalid refuge for homeless squatters. Like all of the park's seven water bodies, the Pond was originally a swamp, artfully shaped into a naturalistic form and filled with subterranean pipes. These Boy Scouts, part of a nature study group, were photographed on Christmas Eve in 1938 playing Santa to the ducks with gifts of bread crumbs. They are perched on a rock outcropping, actually a landscaped concrete shelf on the eastern shore of the Pond.

Above: The Pond's man-made origins would probably come as a surprise to generations of visitors here, including the ducks who have made it their natural habitat. The adjoining woodland is a four-acre bird sanctuary. Easily accessible from the park's main entrance, the scenic Pond is a quiet respite from the nearby midtown business district. Surrounded by steep slopes, it screens out much of the city noise from the major thoroughfares of Fifth Avenue and Fifty-ninth Street only a few blocks away.

GAPSTOW BRIDGE

The bridge has withstood wear and tear for more than a century

Left: Just a few blocks inside the park is one of its most dramatic views. This 1933 photo with boaters looks southeast over the Pond and Gapstow Bridge toward the Plaza Hotel on the right. On the left are two other luxury hotels built in 1927, the Sherry-Netherland and the Savoy, and an office tower, the Squibb Building (1930). The Gapstow in this photo is a rugged stone bridge that crosses the northern neck of the Pond, near East Sixty-third Street. The inset photo shows the original, built in 1874 as a wooden structure with decorative cast-iron railings. The wooden arch did not last very long and was replaced in 1896 by the stone arch.

Above: Like most of the bridges in the park, the Gapstow has withstood wear and tear for more than a century, while the views above the arch have changed substantially. This view looks northeast, the same direction as the archival inset. Although Olmsted and Vaux expected the city to rise up around the park, they did not envision a backdrop of skyscrapers. They intended the bridges to become part of the greenery and designed shrubs and vines to soften their outline. Yet to the modern eye, the contrast of the verdant landscape with the concrete-and-steel city gives the park its unique appeal.

WOLLMAN RINK

The world's largest ice rink when it first opened

Left: Ice-skaters used the park's frozen lake and the Pond for nearly a century until this artificial rink was built in 1950. This is a view of the rink in its first month of operation, January 1951. The 214-by-175-foot rink, the world's largest at the time, was the work of Robert Moses, New York City's powerful parks commissioner from 1934 to 1960. Moses was a driving force for park improvements, but he saw the park as an urban playground with modern, efficiently run recreational facilities, rather than as Olmsted and Vaux's vision of a pastoral pleasure ground. He placed the new rink on a two-acre site just north of the Pond, where it drew harsh criticism for interrupting picturesque views to the north from the Gapstow Bridge. Nonetheless, New Yorkers flocked to the rink, skating day and night while enjoying skyline views of the Plaza Hotel (right) and other midtown buildings.

Above: More than fifty years after the archival photo, the skyline is not the only thing that has changed. While the rink looks much the same, its infrastructure and management have also had some ups and downs. Constant use—not only skating but also summer concerts—cracked its concrete slab and damaged its ice-making system. Park officials demolished the rink in 1980, promising to have a new one up and running in two years. But year after year brought only continued mechanical problems, keeping the rink closed for five winters. In May 1986, Donald Trump, who had completed his first skyscraper, the Trump Tower, two blocks south of the park on Fifth Avenue in 1983, offered to have a new rink working by the winter. He made good on his promise and still manages the popular facility.

THE DAIRY

The park's first "fast-food" restaurant, offering sandwiches, coffee, and ice cream

One of the park's most picturesque structures, the Dairy was built in 1871 as a charming country cottage to dispense fresh milk to visiting children. The ornate loggia, an open gallery, provided a restful place where mothers and children could enjoy summer breezes. To complete the country scene, cows, chickens, and lambs roamed outside. Calvert Vaux designed the building as a Victorian Gothic jewel, similar to the ones he created for the estates of his private clients. Seen here in the early twentieth century, it was part of a group of facilities known as the Children's District in the southern section of the park. Soon after it opened, it became the park's first "fast-food" restaurant, offering sandwiches, coffee, and ice cream.

The Robert Moses era had little use for Gothic jewels. In the depths of the Great Depression that ushered in Moses's first years as city parks commissioner, he secured federal funds to build new playgrounds, but saw no reason to repair the Dairy. The building was relegated to the role of a common warehouse in the 1930s and remained a locked shed for the next half century. Its loggia was destroyed in 1955. The Central Park Conservancy rescued the building in the 1980s, restoring its Gothic gingerbread-house charm. Located a short walk from East Sixty-fifth Street, near the zoo, it looks like an English country church but now serves as a park visitors' center and gift shop.

CHILDREN'S SHELTER

Replaced in 1952 by the Chess and Checkers House

Above: Rustic architecture made of unmilled tree branches was a feature of many eighteenth-century English estates. English architect Calvert Vaux built on this tradition by designing more than a hundred rustic structures throughout the park, including shelters, boat landings, benches, pergolas, beehives, and birdhouses. This one, photographed in 1868, was the largest and most ornate rustic summerhouse in the park. Known as the Children's Shelter, it was located on the Kinderberg, or Children's Mountain, west of the Dairy. This is one of countless stereoscopic photos taken in the park in the 1860s, a time when commercial companies began to market these images to a public entranced by romantic park scenes.

Right: After years of neglect and disrepair, the Children's Shelter was demolished in 1950. It was replaced in 1952 by the brick Chess and Checkers House, but with the focus at first on an older generation. Financier Bernard Baruch donated funds for the building as a refuge for "retired oldsters" after he saw a photograph of old men playing chess on a park bench. In 1984 a wisteria pergola was added, recalling the original rustic shelter and providing a shaded summer spot for the games. Younger players are also encouraged to participate through free chess lessons and the annual Youth Chess Tournament.

VIEW FROM THE
CHILDREN'S SHELTER

Including the Hotel Pierre, the Sherry-Netherland Hotel, and the Squibb Building

From its hilltop setting, the Children's Shelter offered a clear view southeast to Fifth Avenue and Fifty-ninth Street. In this 1932 photo, the rustic branches of the nineteenth-century shelter are framing the fruits of a late-1920s building boom. New York City was in the midst of the Depression when this photo was taken, but the group of elegant buildings visible here comprised a picture of more prosperous times. All of the four towers on the left had been completed just a few years before the photo was taken. From left to right are the Hotel Pierre (1928), the Sherry-Netherland Hotel (1927), the Savoy-Plaza Hotel (1927), and the Squibb Building (1930). On the right is the grande dame of an earlier era, the Plaza Hotel, built in 1907.

The pergola of the Chess and Checkers House, which replaced the rustic shelter in 1952, frames a similar view. Only the Savoy-Plaza Hotel is no longer standing today. It was replaced in 1968 by the General Motors Building, the rectangular hulk in the center. The Plaza Hotel, obscured here by trees, is still going strong, although much larger modern buildings tower over it. The view of the Pond in the archival photo is blocked here by the Wollman Skating Rink, built in 1950.

THE ARSENAL

Exhibits from the American Museum of Natural History were first displayed here

Left: Built in 1848 as a munitions warehouse, the Arsenal (the mock medieval castle in the background) did not figure in the grand plans for the park, but it proved too useful to tear down. After the park was built it became a catchall for a curious mix of things that sound like a schoolboy's wish list: early exhibits of the American Museum of Natural History (which began at the Arsenal), dinosaur models, a weather bureau, and a zoo of sorts. Perhaps because New Yorkers saw the park as a wilderness, they dropped off an odd collection of animals at the Arsenal, conveniently located just off Fifth Avenue at Sixty-fourth Street. Raccoons, foxes, porcupines, eagles, alligators, and even a boa constrictor were kept in cages in the basement. Three buffalo, donated by General William T. Sherman, and a bear, sent from the West by General George Custer, were tied to poles behind the building.

Above: The Arsenal had become a near ruin by the 1920s and was almost torn down. But Robert Moses, who would demolish many original park buildings during his tenure as parks commissioner, found this one useful and preserved it as the Parks Department headquarters. It took on that role in 1934 and has remained so ever since, protected as a city landmark since 1967. (The smaller building on the right in the archival photo no longer exists.) The Arsenal is one of only two Central Park buildings that predate the park. The other is a military blockhouse built for the War of 1812 in a remote section of the park's North Woods. Inside the Arsenal, Olmsted and Vaux's original Greensward plan for Central Park is mounted on the wall of a conference room.

CENTRAL PARK MENAGERIE
IRVING UNDERHILL, 18 PARK PLACE,
NEW YORK
B 10200

THE ZOO

Reopened in 1988 as the Wildlife Conservation Center

Left: A permanent menagerie, seen here in 1903, was built behind the Arsenal in 1870 and led to a dramatic jump in park attendance. In 1873 it attracted 2.5 million visitors, a quarter of all parkgoers that year. Despite the limited space, it had a variety of large animals—hippos, a herd of bison, and elephants, including the one seen here getting a manicure (inset). Conditions deteriorated, however, in the following decades and by the end of the 1920s, the menagerie was a sorry collection of sick animals and rats. In 1934, his first year as parks commissioner, Robert Moses demolished the menagerie and replaced it with a cluster of charming redbrick buildings around a sea lion pool.

Above: By the 1980s, the animal houses and cages built in 1934 were no longer considered charming. Parks commissioner Gordon Davis declared the zoo a "Rikers Island for animals," referring to the city's notorious jail. The new zoo, opened in 1988, came with a new name, the Wildlife Conservation Center, and a new philosophy of humane habitats. Its buildings, connected by a graceful arcade, replicate a rain forest, temperate zone, and polar region. Elephants, gorillas, and most other big animals are no longer here, having found a new home in the much larger Bronx Zoo. But polar bears, penguins, seals, and even snow leopards now cavort in Central Park's more commodious quarters. Unfortunately, humans have to pay an entrance fee to the new zoo, the first for-pay facility in the otherwise all-free park.

CHILDREN'S ZOO

The zoo's colorful fiberglass animals were replaced by an environmentally conscious play area in 1997

Left: This lighthearted addition to the main zoo was built in 1961, the year of this photo. It was populated by a collection of whimsical figures, including a child-sized Noah's Ark and a fiberglass whale, affectionately known as Whaleamena. But even this fairyland could not withstand economic reality. The roller-coaster waves of economic recession in the 1970s and late 1980s imposed a heavy toll on park maintenance and finally closed the Children's Zoo in 1992. Whaleamena was shipped off to Rockaway Beach in Queens, but had her tail sliced off to fit in the delivery truck, among other humiliating damages. She was restored by a volunteer Parks Department employee and now presides on the ocean boardwalk.

Right: The zoo's cartoonlike characters were not only in bad shape in the 1990s, but also were derided as kitsch. While new designs proposed a more sophisticated environment, nostalgic baby boomers who had grown up visiting the old zoo strongly protested its demolition. They were overruled, however, and in 1997 the new zoo opened as an environmentally conscious enchanted forest, albeit one with plastic trees. It provides active play for young children, who can crawl through gargantuan tree trunks or pretend to be spiders by climbing over a large net.

BALTO MEMORIAL

Honoring the Alaskan sled dog who saved thousands of lives in 1925

Left: As strange as it may seem to erect a statue of an Alaskan sled dog in a New York City park, Balto's heroic trek captured the public's imagination in 1925. That year he led a team of huskies through a blinding blizzard on a five-day, nearly 700-mile final run to deliver diphtheria antitoxin to Nome, Alaska, saving thousands of lives. Balto and his teammates went to Hollywood to star in a film about the journey, and Balto dog food was soon on the market. The larger-than-life statue stands on a rock pedestal northwest of the Children's Zoo, near East Sixty-seventh Street. The real dog attended the unveiling of his statue in 1925, but was reportedly unimpressed. In this 1933 photo, a group of young mushers have hitched their sleds to the star.

Above: Balto now has a golden sheen burnished by generations of children climbing and stroking the bronze statue during its more than eight decades in the park. Olmsted and Vaux discouraged statuary in the park, but failed to resist the public pressure for it that mounted almost immediately. The city's large German American community managed to erect the first piece of sculpture, a bust of the poet Johann von Schiller, in 1859, just a year after the start of park construction. Many other ethnic groups followed their lead. Today there are fifty-one sculptures in the park. While proposals for more arise from time to time, they are not encouraged.

FIFTH AVENUE AND
SIXTY-SEVENTH STREET

Crowds gather for the wedding of Anna Gould and Count Boni de Castellane in 1895

The crowds that gathered here on March 4, 1895, in front of a mansion facing Central Park had come to gawk at the celebrated guests arriving for one of the most talked-about weddings of the day. Anna Gould, daughter of the fabulously wealthy Jay Gould—financier, railroad developer, and, so everyone said, a notorious robber baron—was marrying Count Boni de Castellane, the bearer of an old French title but very little fortune. Fifth Avenue mansions provided a ready supply of American heiresses eager for European titles, particularly those looking to put a shine on a shady family name. The bare trees of the park on this early spring day were a sign of a cold future for this marriage of convenience.

Neither the marriage nor the mansion had a lasting future. The couple divorced in 1906, after the count put a dent in the Gould fortune through gambling and various other entertainments. Anna Gould, after marrying another French noble—one with his own money—eventually gave up living in mansions and spent her final days as a widow surrounded by bodyguards and nurses in a grand suite at the Plaza Hotel. The site of her first wedding, a château built by her brother George Gould, went the way of nearly every palatial home built on Fifth Avenue in the nineteenth century. It was replaced by a wave of new apartment buildings like this one; forty buildings alone were constructed in the 1920s.

THE MALL—LITERARY WALK

Lined with statues of famous writers, including Walter Scott and Robert Burns

Left: Modeled on the grand *allées* of European parks, the Mall is both a formal exception to the naturalistic park and the park's masterpiece. Designed to be the only straight line in the curvilinear park, it culminates at the terrace and Bethesda Fountain, opening to a breathtaking vista of the lake (see pages 50–51). By setting the Mall within a lush green landscape, the park designers made a traditional feature all the more impressive. This is a circa-1905 view of the Mall's southern end, located midpark off East Sixty-seventh Street. It is known as the Literary Walk because several statues of famous poets and writers line the walkway. Two nineteenth-century favorites, Sir Walter Scott on the right and Robert Burns on the left, were dedicated in 1880.

Above: The statues of Scott and Burns are still sheltered by the Mall's most striking feature—its thick canopy of trees. Four rows of elms with branches reaching fifty feet high form a living cathedral along the quarter-mile-long Mall. Most of the original trees died after the first year of planting due to subsoil problems, and many of the replacements were lost due to the spread of Dutch elm disease in the 1930s. Replanting and constant horticultural maintenance has preserved 150. These towering survivors and the two and a half miles of elms along the park's Fifth Avenue border are the largest stands of American elms in North America. Although a devastating storm in August 2009 felled more than 100 trees in the park, these particular trees survived once again.

THE MALL—NORTHERN END

An urban promenade, a place to socialize, to see and be seen

Above: The Mall has always functioned as an urban promenade, a place to socialize, to see and be seen. Although it tested racial and class tensions within the growing metropolis, it changed as the city did, accommodating an increasingly multicultural and economically diverse population. To the right of center in this 1902 photo is a cast-iron music pavilion where free concerts were held. In the 1860s and 1870s, influential groups within the city's Protestant majority convinced park officials to prohibit concerts on Sundays, effectively closing off these events to the working class whose only day off was on Sunday. The rules were relaxed in the 1880s, although everyone still dressed up for the occasion.

Right: The nineteenth-century music pavilion was replaced by a 1920s band shell on the other side of the Mall (left), but the activity all around it is timeless. More than a century after the archival photo, the only other difference on this early spring day is the change from Victorian to contemporary dress. While people no longer get dressed up to join the promenade, they still come here to enjoy the scene, walking between the towering elms to see the newly emerging leaves, pushing baby carriages or stopping at the refreshment stand for a hot dog. Caught up in different worlds, they nonetheless share a common pleasure in strolling through the park.

NAUMBURG BAND SHELL

Where 50,000 people gathered on December 14, 1980, to pay tribute to John Lennon

Left: In 1923 the original music stand in the Mall was replaced by this neoclassical band shell, a gift of banker Elkan Naumburg, who donated it to the city "and its music lovers." No doubt, he would have been surprised to see the gathering photographed here on December 14, 1980, the day John Lennon was shot and killed. The event was an impromptu response to the former Beatle's murder in front of his nearby home on Central Park West and Seventy-second Street. The crowd of some 50,000 people maintained a silent vigil while Lennon's music was played over the sound system. The band shell had been a venue for traditional music concerts from 1923 until 1969, when rock groups also began to perform. Neighborhood complaints about the noise level and rowdy behavior led to new park rules in the 1980s prohibiting hard rock.

Above: In 1989 city and park officials proposed demolishing the concrete-and-limestone band shell and returning the area, which had been cleared of trees and paved with asphalt in 1923, to greener surroundings. Park and preservation organizations did not protest tearing down the band shell, but the Naumburg family was outraged. The donor's great-grandson led a campaign against the demolition, ultimately stopping it in the courts in 1993. While the area around it was improved, the band shell holds its ground. It still hosts impromptu gatherings and occasional performances, subject to the noise regulations. A permanent "Imagine" memorial to Lennon (inset) was created on the west side of the park in 1985. The landscape around it is named for another Lennon song, "Strawberry Fields Forever."

CASINO

Demolished in 1934, the site is now home to the Rumsey Playfield

Built as the Ladies' Refreshment Salon in 1864, this building near the northern end of the Mall was transformed in 1929 to become the Central Park Casino, a pet project of Mayor James J. Walker and his Broadway showgirl companion. Walker secured a low-rent lease for one of his friends who, with the mayor's encouragement, spent $400,000 to change the building into a glittering nightclub. The transformation was the work of Joseph Urban, an Austrian architect who also designed theatrical sets for the Metropolitan Opera and Ziegfeld Follies and lavish interiors for Palm Beach mansions. The domed pavilion was an addition to what had been a modest cottage. The private upstairs suite was the mayor's unofficial city hall, where he held court for politicians and favor-seekers. The women in the inset are waitresses in costume for a special event at the Casino.

Despite its name, the Casino was not a gambling venue but a high-priced dinner club where guests danced in a mirrored ballroom and enjoyed bootleg liquor during Prohibition. But to political reformers during the Great Depression, it was a scandalous stain on a public park. Once Mayor Fiorello La Guardia took office in 1934, his newly appointed parks commissioner, Robert Moses, demolished the building. Politically correct for the day, the action robbed the city of a great work by Joseph Urban and a lovely park building by Calvert Vaux. Its replacement was the Rumsey Playfield, an open area used for sports and other seasonal activities, such as SummerStage, a venue for outdoor concerts.

UPPER TERRACE

A favorite gathering place for New Yorkers and visitors

Left: The bilevel terrace, Calvert Vaux's architectural masterpiece, is considered the heart of Central Park. In Vaux's own words, "The landscape is everything, the architecture nothing—til you get to the Terrace." The upper level begins where the Mall ends, at this landing, seen in 1942. Looking northwest from the center of the park at Seventy-second Street, it provides a sweeping view of the lower terrace, Bethesda Fountain, the lake, and the distant trees of the wooded ramble. The architectural elements, masterfully integrated within the landscape, were among the first structures built in the park. Construction began in 1859, just months after the lake was excavated and filled in December 1858.

Above: Wonderfully scenic as it was from the start, the expansive view from the upper terrace is all the more inspiring within a city as dense as New York. This is a favorite gathering place for New Yorkers and visitors, including the group shown here, who are just as pleased to have their picture taken as the two women in the 1942 photo. Although the scene looks much the same in the two photos, the intervening years brought dramatic changes to this site. It was hardly recognizable in the 1970s when the terrace and fountain were seriously damaged and defaced by vandalism. Thanks to an ambitious restoration program begun in the 1980s, this beautiful spot once again reflects the designers' vision.

COPYRIGHT 1894 BY J.S. JOHNSTON,

TERRACE STEPS

One of two massive flights of steps between the upper and lower terrace

This 1894 view looking south reveals the seamless connection between the upper terrace and the Mall with its canopy of trees. This is one of two massive flights of stairs leading down to both sides of the lower terrace. Construction slowed during the first years of the Civil War but remained a high priority for the park designers. Calvert Vaux pressed the cost-conscious park officials to use expensive sandstone to face the staircases, railings, and posts. Vaux's talented assistant, Jacob Wrey Mould, embellished them with intricate carvings, including unique arabesques depicting the seasons with birds, insects, and plants.

While it would seem that only clothing styles have changed over the past century, this beautiful staircase has been through extreme changes of its own. Gouged and covered with graffiti in the 1970s, the carvings were renewed as part of the restoration program mounted by the Central Park Conservancy in 1983. Artists recarved lost birds' heads and other features of the ornamented stonework. Today, the handcrafted staircase is just as scenic and popular as it was in the 1890s.

LOWER TERRACE

Calvert Vaux's design allowed all New Yorkers to enjoy
the splendor of a royal estate in their own backyard

Above: The full expanse of the lower terrace is displayed in this 1902 panoramic photo. Largely completed even before the end of the Civil War in 1864, it was a magnificent achievement. Vaux considered it his finest work and took pride in the fact that it allowed all New Yorkers to enjoy the splendor of a royal estate in their own backyard. It offered both sweeping vistas and exquisite details. Its focal point is the Bethesda Fountain in the center of the photo. On the right, between two beautifully carved stone staircases is a gracefully arched arcade, the dramatic terminus of a tunnel leading from the Mall under the Seventy-second Street drive.

Right: By the 1980s, the terrace was in near-ruin. Chunks of stonework were missing from the stairways and fountain walls. The sloping lawns were barren areas of compacted dirt. With infusions of private funds to the park's budget, the Central Park Conservancy conducted an exhaustive four-year restoration. The terrace and fountain were dismantled and rebuilt with new stone quarried from the original sources. The entire area was landscaped with new lawns and flowering shrubs. Careful maintenance has kept it all in splendid form.

This photo, taken in 1942, looks down from one of the terrace staircases to the arches opening to the terrace arcade. Sailors on leave from World War II duty are enjoying the terrace café, a casual retreat within an elaborately decorated setting. Just inside the arches is a vaulted ceiling covered with 16,000 Minton tiles designed by Jacob Wrey Mould. Manufactured in England, each tile was richly colored and glazed with intricate patterns reminiscent of those in the Alhambra in Spain.

TERRACE ARCADE

The vaulted ceiling is covered with 16,000 Minton tiles designed by Jacob Wrey Mould

A more upscale alfresco café opened here in the 1960s, but the kitchen facilities were tucked under the arcade and blocked that dramatic entranceway from the Mall to the lower terrace and fountain. The café closed in 1972 at the height of drug trafficking in the area. During this period of neglected maintenance, water seeped into the arcade's vaulted ceiling and corroded the plates holding the Minton tiles. They were removed in the 1980s and kept in storage for decades. After restoration funds were finally available, the tiles were painstakingly repaired by hand and reinstalled in 2007 (inset). The terrace arcade is often used as an elegant setting for wedding photos.

ANGEL OF THE WATERS /
BETHESDA FOUNTAIN

Now an elegant symbol of the park's resurgence

Calvert Vaux intended to place several allegorical sculptures on the terrace, but this was the only one commissioned from the park's original design. The bronze figure of the angel was created by Emma Stebbins, the first woman to receive a commission for a major public work in New York City. Dedicated in 1873, it celebrates the opening of the Croton Aqueduct, which first brought freshwater to the city in 1842. Seen here in 1892, the angel blesses the water of the fountain with one hand and carries a lily, a symbol of purity, in the other. Stebbins was inspired by a biblical passage describing an angel who bestowed healing powers on the pool of Bethesda in Jerusalem. Hence it became known as the Bethesda Fountain.

Always a gathering place, the fountain became a hangout for countercultural youth in the 1960s and 1970s. Dubbed "Freak Fountain" by a *Newsweek* article, it was derided by conservative voices and celebrated by others, particularly fashion editors who went there to observe the latest hippie trends. Vandalism, made worse by neglect during the city's fiscal crisis of the 1970s, left the fountain in desperate need of repair. In the 1980s, the Central Park Conservancy repaired the bluestone walls and cleaned, repainted, and resealed the fountain with a protective coating. Washed and waxed annually, it is an elegant symbol of the park's resurgence. The Bethesda Fountain is a key scene in Tony Kushner's award-winning play *Angels in America*, which debuted on Broadway in 1993.

J.S. JOHNSTON
EW & MARINE PHOTO

LAKE AND BETHESDA FOUNTAIN

"The Bride of Venice" gondola can still be reserved for special occasions

Left: The butterfly-shaped lake spreads across twenty-two acres following a twisting, turning shoreline north of the Seventy-second Street drive. The eastern wing overlooking the Bethesda Fountain is particularly scenic, made all the more picturesque by the gondola in this circa-1900 photo. In the nineteenth century, private boatmen circled the lake, picking up and dropping off passengers at six landings. One could take a six- or twelve-seat boat, or a gondola poled by one of the authentic Venetian gondoliers who serenaded passengers with Italian arias. The inset shows a group of the gondoliers in the original boathouse.

Above: One gondola, named "the Bride of Venice," still plies the lake waters by special reservation. Otherwise, boating is mostly a do-it-yourself activity today. Rowboats can be rented at the boathouse on the eastern side of the lake and boaters can stop at one of four remaining boat landings. Many visitors choose to walk around the shoreline, exploring its hidden inlets or simply gazing at the changing scenery of open vistas, overhanging trees, and the city skyline. Like the archival photo, this view was taken from the Point, a promontory in the wooded ramble north of the lake.

LAKE BOATHOUSE

Rebuilt as the Loeb Boathouse in 1954

Left: This 1904 photo looks east toward the park's first boathouse, built in 1873. The rustic, two-story structure was a lovely place to board a boat or just watch the activity on the water from the second deck. By the turn of the century, many New Yorkers were rowing their own boats, much like today, but in dressier attire. Excursion boats were also available for hire, like the one with a canopy docked at the boathouse. A new boathouse came on the scene in 1954. This long, low structure with redbrick walls, white limestone trim, and a swooping copper-clad roof was a gift of investment banker Carl Loeb. Ten years later, on a snowy February day in 1964, the Beatles (inset) posed for publicity photos at the Loeb Boathouse during their first visit to New York City.

Above: Today, lakeside dining is as much of an attraction as boating was in the nineteenth century. The Loeb Boathouse offers a variety of venues, a high-end restaurant with a waterfront terrace, a cafeteria, café, and bar. People-watching is part of the attraction, but this is also a gathering place for birdwatchers, who come here to record the birds seen in the park in a central listing.

LAKE VIEW EAST

Looking toward the forty-story Carlyle Hotel, built in 1930

Left: The trees were just showing new leaves on this warm spring day in 1934 when boaters came out on the park lake. They had an uninterrupted view of the newest tower on Manhattan's East Side skyline, the forty-story Carlyle Hotel, built in 1930 on Madison Avenue and East Seventy-sixth Street. Some critics compared it to the bell tower of London's Westminster Cathedral; others thought it looked like a "gigantic screw-plug" for an electric lightbulb. At its feet is the massive dome of Temple Beth-El on Fifth Avenue and Seventy-sixth Street. It was the city's grandest synagogue when built in 1891, and was the first house of worship to face Central Park.

Above: Spring has had the same effect on New Yorkers for the past half century, drawing people to the park and dotting the lake with boaters. While the East Side skyline has changed somewhat, the Carlyle Hotel is still in the picture at left. It was President John F. Kennedy's favorite hotel in New York City in the early 1960s. However, Temple Beth-El is gone. It was demolished in 1947, years after the congregation moved into the new Temple Emanu-El at Fifth Avenue and Sixty-fifth Street, the site of the former Astor mansion.

CONSERVATORY WATER

Still a popular gathering place for model sailboat clubs

Left: Called the Conservatory Water for a promised but never built greenhouse on this spot, the pond was meant to be a reflecting pool for the glass conservatories. Instead, it became a favorite place for model sailboat clubs. In this 1917 photo, boys are propelling the sailboats with long sticks and hoping for a strong wind. Future generations would gather at the pond in coming years to race sailboats, motorized speedboats, and model ocean liners. Stuart Little, a fictional mouse small enough to fit on his model boat, piloted it to victory here in E. B. White's 1945 children's story of the same name.

Above: This sailor has a more specialized stick to push off his craft, but he also has a remote-control device to keep it going without any wind. Stuart Little sailed his boat on the pond once again in the 1999 movie version about the intrepid mouse who also had to fend off hawks cruising for wildlife in the area. Fortunately, he did not have to do battle with the real-life hawks, Pale Male and Lola, who have nested for years on the twelfth floor of the apartment tower just east of the pond on Fifth Avenue near Seventy-fourth Street, a convenient launch for hunting forays into the park. The hawks became famous in 2004 when their nest was removed as a nuisance to the luxury apartment dwellers. After a public outcry, it was restored, happily allowing the birdwatchers who gather at the pond to continue their observations.

TREFOIL ARCH

Built in 1862 to continue the pathway under the East Drive near Seventy-fourth Street

Above: The arch gets its name from the three-lobed shape framing its entrance. The design is on just one side; the other has a simple rounded opening, an unusual two-faced design. The facing, made of brownstone, ubiquitous in New York row houses, is also unusual for the park, as most of the others are of New Brunswick sandstone. One of the park's early arches, it was built in 1862 to continue the pathway under the East Drive near Seventy-fourth Street. In those days without traffic lights, it allowed pedestrians, like this woman with her baby carriage, to walk safely under the drive without encountering horse-drawn carriages.

Right: Now that the East Drive regularly carries heavy automobile traffic, the Trefoil Arch is an even more important passageway. It provides a safe pedestrian link between two popular park attractions, the Conservatory Water and the Loeb Boathouse. A steady stream of people often pass through it. This is the distinctive eastern facade featuring the trefoil opening flanked by quatrefoils in round frames. The simpler round opening on the other side can be seen in silhouette through the tunnel.

Byron, N.Y.

OBELISK

This 244-ton granite monolith dating to 1461 BC was shipped over from Egypt in 1880

Left: Thousands of years old, seventy-one feet high, and covered with ancient hieroglyphics, the obelisk was a fascinating attraction to park visitors in the late nineteenth century. The Egyptian pharaoh Thutmosis III had a pair of them made to celebrate the thirtieth year of his reign in 1461 BC. One was shipped to London in 1879 to stand on the bank of the Thames. William H. Vanderbilt believed that New York City deserved one of its own—so passionately that he paid for its amazing journey from Egypt. The 244-ton granite monolith was lowered onto a ship in Egypt (inset) in 1880 to sail across the Mediterranean Sea and the Atlantic Ocean—a feat that was relatively easy compared to the four months it took to transport it from the banks of the Hudson River to the park. Thousands of people stood in the snow on January 22, 1881, the year of this photo, to see the obelisk turned upright.

Above: On days when the park is closed to autos, the drive past the obelisk is not much different than in the archival photo, except, of course, for the runners. The obelisk is often called "Cleopatra's Needle," although she had nothing to do with its creation, which took place about a thousand years before her birth. Its ancient heritage was often entwined with historic fantasy. In his film *The Ten Commandments*, director Cecil B. DeMille portrayed the raising of an obelisk similar to the actual event that took place in the park. DeMille played in the park as a boy and in 1956, the year the film was released (his original silent version was in 1923), he donated funds for a plaque on the park's obelisk translating the hieroglyphics, which recount the reign of Thutmosis III.

METROPOLITAN MUSEUM OF ART

Its location in Central Park has been stirring controversy for over a century

Left: The placement of the Metropolitan Museum of Art in Central Park was controversial from the institution's founding in 1867. Olmsted objected to the intrusion of buildings into the park's naturalistic setting. In turn, some of the museum founders feared that the location at Fifth Avenue and Eighty-first Street was too remote from the city's center to attract visitors. Nevertheless, the first building, designed by Calvert Vaux to blend into the park, opened in 1880 (inset). By the time of the circa-1914 photo, Vaux's building was no longer visible, having been engulfed by several additions: a Greco-Roman entrance pavilion built by Richard Morris Hunt in 1895 and the first of McKim, Mead, and White's classical wings along Fifth Avenue to the right. The building on the left behind Hunt's pavilion was added in 1888 by Theodore Weston. The obelisk can be seen in the distance on the far left.

Above: After a century-long series of additions, the monumental museum stands like a Versailles palace in Central Park. Following the developments apparent in the archival photo, the museum's growing collections and popularity led to further expansion plans, as well as controversies and lawsuits in the late 1960s and early 1970s about its continued encroachment on the park. Since 1974 six new wings have been added. The most dramatic departure from the classical was the glass-enclosed Sackler Wing in 1978. Hidden by the last visible building on the right, it is a serene showcase for the ancient Egyptian Temple of Dendur that once stood on the banks of the Nile. The Metropolitan contains the most comprehensive art collection in the Western Hemisphere. Although the museum bears little relationship to the park, they stand together as two of New York City's greatest treasures.

CONSERVATORY GARDEN

The grand Victorian greenhouses became a victim of 1930s thrift

These greenhouses were built near Fifth Avenue and 105th Street in 1898. The Mount St. Vincent Convent once stood on a hillside directly behind the site. The nuns moved to the Bronx in the 1860s and Olmsted lived in the convent with his family while he supervised construction of the park. In 1883 a nearby tavern became the Mount St. Vincent Restaurant, but when it turned into a drinking haunt for rowdy Tammany Hall politicians, the nuns complained that their good name was being besmirched and so the name was changed. Anti-Tammany officials demolished the building in 1915. The greenhouses continued to serve as plant nurseries for the park and for flower shows.

Considered too high-maintenance during the Great Depression, the greenhouses were torn down in 1934 to make way for the Conservatory Garden, designed by the appropriately named Betty Sprout. Although it lost the greenhouses, it gained a pair of monumental iron gates at the entrance. Forged in Paris in 1894, they formerly stood before the Cornelius Vanderbilt II mansion at Fifth Avenue and Fifty-eighth Street (see pages 8–9) and were donated by his daughter, Gloria Vanderbilt Whitney, after the mansion was demolished in 1926. The garden was beautifully restored in the 1990s. This view looks through the gates to the central lawn and fountain. A curving wisteria pergola nestles into the hillside at the rear of the garden.

WEST 110TH STREET AND CENTRAL PARK WEST

At one time you could see two very different trains in the park

Left: New York City's first elevated railway ran along the northwest corner of the park on a trestle 100 feet in the air. It began in 1868 in Lower Manhattan and by the late nineteenth century extended northward along Ninth Avenue until the park's northern end at 110th Street. As seen here, it turned sharply onto Central Park West (Eighth Avenue) to continue north into Harlem. In the foreground of this circa-1900 photo, horses are pulling a wagon across the snow-covered meadow of the still largely undeveloped corner of the park. Through the trestle on the right one can see part of Morningside Park, also designed by Olmsted and Vaux, and, on the right horizon, the massive St. Luke's Hospital. The inset photo shows the miniature railroad, the "Limited Express," that ran in the park in 1904.

Above: While subway lines began to tunnel through Manhattan about the time of the archival photo, the Ninth Avenue elevated trestle lasted until 1940. Today the view from this corner of the park is completely blocked by apartment buildings that went up in the 1980s, providing affordable housing for this section of Harlem. The center area is Frederick Douglass Circle, dedicated in 1950 and now under reconstruction. When completed, it will include a statue of Douglass, the escaped slave who became a world-renowned orator and abolitionist. It will also memorialize the Underground Railroad that led slaves to freedom.

TENNIS COURTS

The park once sported 200 tennis courts during the summer

Left: Introduced to America in the 1870s, the game of tennis was enormously popular by the time grass courts were opened in the park in 1885. More than 200 courts like these photographed in 1896 (inset) were simply outlined with chalk and set up with temporary netting on the park meadows. In 1912 they were replaced by twenty-nine permanent courts near the West Ninety-sixth Street entrance to the park (main picture). A New York Times article in 1914 reported that the new courts were used by 700 people on a single Sunday and that in good weather, between 3,000 and 10,000 people gathered to watch the games. The building in the left background is the North Gate House, built in the 1880s as a pumping station for the Upper Reservoir.

Above: By 1927 the Tennis Center included thirty courts, the same number in use today. Players began calling for a field house with lockers and showers. The Tennis House (left) was built in 1930 and despite calls for a replacement, it remains virtually unchanged today. Park and city officials supported the plan for a new building that would be more in keeping with the naturalistic park landscape than the old neoclassical building. But like several other recent proposals to demolish and replace a park structure, the plan to tear down the old Tennis House and build a new pavilion became controversial and quietly died. The North Gate House still stands behind the Tennis House but is no longer in use.

GOTHIC BRIDGE

One of five cast-iron bridges restored by city engineers

One of five cast-iron bridges in the park—most of the other three dozen are masonry—the Gothic Bridge is the most distinctive. The spandrels on either side of the graceful arch look like Gothic windows, hence the eventual name for the bridge, which was originally called simply "Bridge No. 28." It was built in 1864 and—like all of the park bridges—skillfully carried pathways over other roads; in this case, a bridle path along the northern edge of the Upper Reservoir. By the 1970s, when this photo was taken, runners had become more common than equestrians in the park. In 1970 the finish line for the New York City Marathon was placed in Central Park, making it all the more attractive to the increasing numbers of runners each year.

Covered with rust by the 1970s, the cast iron had to be thoroughly overhauled and checked for flaws. But before the work could begin, the original construction process had to be examined. City engineers found the original drawings and prepared new ones for the iron workers. They completed the repairs in 1983, carefully grinding down the iron until its curved outlines were as crisp as they were in 1864. Although equestrian traffic is not heavy enough today to demand a bridge, it remains a delightful addition to the landscape and an elegant passageway for pedestrians.

GREAT LAWN

The Great Depression saw the rise of "Hooverville" in a drained reservoir

Left: During the depth of the Great Depression, Central Park's pastoral landscape became the setting for a shocking scene of harsh economic reality. More than 200 shacks were built by the homeless in the former Lower Reservoir, which had been drained in 1929. The site had a history of hard times. Nearly a century earlier, it had been part of Seneca Village, a small but established settlement of African Americans who were displaced by the building of the reservoir in 1842 and ultimately by the park in 1859. While widespread unemployment in the 1930s led to many other "Hoovervilles," named for Herbert Hoover, president at the start of the Depression, the one in Central Park was the most famous, a graphic symbol of the nation's despair. This is a 1931 view looking east toward Fifth Avenue. In the far right background is the original version of the Metropolitan Museum of Art (see page 72 inset).

Above: The Hooverville squatters were dispersed in 1933 and most of the reservoir land was then filled with rubble from the Rockefeller Center excavation. The pond in the foreground, now a wildlife sanctuary called Turtle Pond, is the only reminder that the entire site was once underwater. (A later, larger reservoir still exists directly to the north.) The pond adjoins the thirteen-acre Great Lawn, surrounded by playgrounds and baseball diamonds, visible on the left. In later years, the lawn hosted hugely popular events, from the Simon and Garfunkel reunion concert in 1980 to an outdoor Mass celebrated by Pope John Paul II in 1995. By then, the lawn had become a dust bowl and was closed for two years for restoration. It reopened in 1997, but with a fence and strict rules limiting public use. The only regular events are annual performances by the Metropolitan Opera and the New York Philharmonic Orchestra.

DELACORTE THEATER

With a castle view beyond, the Delacorte Theater has the perfect backdrop for Shakespeare

Above: Robert Moses made a huge legal and public relations blunder when he banned the free Shakespeare performances in the park in 1959, demanding that the founder, Joseph Papp, charge admission in order to pay $10,000 to the Parks Department to cover the cost of replacing the grass. Papp refused and took his case to court, which decided in his favor, calling Moses "clearly arbitrary, capricious, and unreasonable." In a complete reversal, Moses built a permanent amphitheater for the performances in 1962, with much of the funding provided by Dell Publishing founder George T. Delacorte. Located southwest of the Great Lawn, it is seen here in 1964 during a performance of *Hamlet*. The view looks southeast over Turtle Pond.

Right: In 1974 the city and Joseph Papp announced plans to build a new theater to replace the deteriorating Delacorte. Coming in the midst of the city's fiscal crisis, the estimated construction cost of $3 million was criticized as irresponsible. The city withdrew the proposal, but Papp was ultimately successful in raising $1 million in private funds to renovate the Delacorte in 1976. This is a view of the entire theater today, looking down from Belvedere Castle. The popular performances often include film and stage stars such as Kevin Kline, Denzel Washington, and Meryl Streep in leading roles. New Yorkers and tourists line up for hours to secure the free tickets on a first-come, first-served basis.

BELVEDERE CASTLE

A folly in the grand tradition

Left: "Belvedere" means "beautiful view" in Italian—the perfect name for a place built to see and be seen. Perched atop Vista Rock, the highest point in the park, just north of the Seventy-ninth Street transverse road, the castle was a viewing platform overlooking the Lower Reservoir to the north. Directly on line with the long axis of the Mall, it was meant to be seen as a romantic focal point for views from Bethesda Terrace. Its intentionally small scale lengthened the perspective, making the intervening distance appear greater from many parts of the park. It was designed by Calvert Vaux and built in 1872. This is a circa-1900 view of one end of the castle.

Right: The castle's elevated position made it an ideal weather station, but its peaked roof was flattened to accommodate meteorological instruments in the 1930s. It also endured years of vandalism and graffiti. Its profile was restored in a total makeover in the 1980s, and it was rehabilitated once again in 1996 with new windows and doors to make way for the Henry Luce Learning Center, featuring exhibits and programs on the park's natural environment. It also continues as a data-gathering outpost for the U.S. Weather Bureau, providing the familiar New York City report on the weather in Central Park. Although intervening treetops block the distant view of the castle from Bethesda Terrace, it remains one of the most picturesque structures in the park.

RAMBLE STONE ARCH

This tiny arch was part of Olmsted's plan to create a sense of mystery in the park

Above: Opening like a keyhole through rustic stone blocks, this is the narrowest arch in the park and one of the most unusual. Only five feet wide, it fills a crevice between two large boulders set within the Ramble, an artfully contrived wilderness. The arch, built in 1863, is in the northwest corner of the Ramble, which lies between Belvedere Castle and the lake. Since carriage drives did not penetrate this rocky, wooded landscape, the arch, unlike others in the park, did not have to solve traffic problems. It simply adds to the atmosphere for people walking on the footpaths above and below. Thickly forested, the area looked more like a place for Druids than for the group here in Victorian dress.

Right: If the group in the archival photo were transported here, they would notice hardly any difference in the scene. The picturesque arch, made up largely of boulders found in the park, has been beautifully preserved. Olmsted wanted the Ramble—which includes thirty-seven acres of woodlands, marshland, a stream, a waterfall, and even a cave—to create a sense of mystery. This arch and the cave just steps away were part of that fanciful atmosphere. Known as the Indian Cave, it was a major attraction in the nineteenth century, but was closed off in the 1920s. Nonetheless, visitors who pass through this rustic stone arch can still feel that they are far from civilization.

RAMBLE GORGE

Engineers gave nature a helping hand to create one of the best bird-watching sites in the country

As natural as it looks, this rocky setting is another man-made part of the Ramble. While the designers laid out meandering paths around existing rock outcroppings, they also moved huge boulders to create scenes like this one, photographed in 1905. Surprisingly, they took on this arduous task as one of the first park projects, opening Ramble pathways in 1859, just a year after the start of construction. While the industrial revolution was gaining steam in this period, retreats to natural settings became increasingly popular. Resorts were built in the Catskill and Adirondack mountains north of the city, but settings like these in Central Park brought nature close to home.

Hikers still enjoy the Ramble's wild atmosphere despite the efforts of Robert Moses, who liked his parks clean and tidy. In 1955 he planned to widen some of the narrow pathways for horseshoe pitching, shuffleboard, and croquet. The proposal raised a howl of protest and was ultimately defeated, primarily by bird-watchers who had discovered a birding haven in the wilds of the Ramble. Over the years, the Ramble became overgrown and truly wild. In 1981 the newly formed Central Park Conservancy cleared away brush and dead wood, but when they cut down some trees to reclaim the view between Belvedere Castle and Bethesda Terrace, bird-watchers throughout the city were outraged. The Audubon Society has ranked the Ramble as one of the top fifteen bird-watching locales in the entire country, along with Yosemite and the Everglades.

GILL BRIDGE

Where the Gill meets the lake, by West Seventy-sixth Street

Left: The Gill, Scottish for "spring," begins in the Ramble, where it is fed by water from the park reservoir through a pipe buried deep in the rocks. Here, at the western edge of the Ramble, the gurgling spring reaches the shoreline of the lake opposite West Seventy-sixth Street. The wooden railing is part of the Gill Bridge, one of six small rustic bridges built in the park. This 1932 photo looks southwest over the lake toward the apartment buildings on Central Park West. The twin-towered ones on the right (San Remo) and left (Majestic) were built just two years before the photo. In between are two lower buildings from an earlier era: the Dakota (1884) on the left, and the Langham (1905).

Above: Vulnerable to vandalism, the wooden bridge was destroyed several times over the years. Its replacement is a more durable modern version. More trees have grown in the Ramble, partially blocking the view of Central Park West. But with one or two modern exceptions, the view of the skyline from this picturesque spot has changed little since the 1930s. This scene has been preserved thanks to the protection the distinctive buildings have received through the city's Landmarks Preservation Commission.

BOW BRIDGE

A reluctant addition by Olmsted and Vaux has become a beloved icon

Left: Shaped like an archer's bow, this graceful bridge spans the pinched point between the two butterfly wings of the lake and connects the Ramble to the Lower Terrace and the Bethesda Fountain. This early twentieth-century view looks toward the forested shoreline of the Ramble. Olmsted and Vaux were reluctant to make the connection because they wanted strollers to discover the Ramble slowly through pathways around either end of the lake. Bowing to pressure from a park commissioner, they built this low-lying bridge in 1862.

Above: By the early 1970s, the bridge's stone abutments were crumbling and its ironwork was eroding. A 1972 article in the *New Yorker* magazine said the once glorious bridge looked "as if it had been mugged," a reference to the frequency of actual muggings in the park during this period of neglected security and maintenance. Private funds were raised to make the necessary repairs in 1974, and in 1998 it got a new walkway and new paint in its original colors of beige and white. Large planting urns at either end of the bridge, missing for nearly a century, were finally replaced in 2008. Ironically, the bridge Olmsted and Vaux had to be persuaded to build has become a beloved icon of Central Park.

By the 1920s, the Victorian concept of the park as a romantic wilderness was fading, but park officials found new ways to promote it. This 1927 photo identifies the Native American in the canoe as "Chief Great Fire of the Iroquois," appointed by the city parks commissioner as "general custodian and guardian around Central Park Lake." Paddling under the Bow Bridge, he appears to be an authentic vestige of the Old West, but the truth was more prosaic. Born on an Indian reservation in Canada, Chief Great Fire lived in Brooklyn.

BOW BRIDGE

Chief Great Fire of the Iroquois in his role as general custodian and guardian

Without any actors or props, the Bow Bridge still creates an illusion of the romantic past. Seemingly poured over the lake, its span is exquisitely laced with Greek and Gothic details. Its graceful exterior hides an engineering feat of the nineteenth century. The stone abutments rest on an unusual foundation—cannonballs—which act as movable bearings, allowing the cast-iron span to expand and contract in changing weather conditions. "For its grace, prominence, and renown," according to the *New York Times*, "it may be thought of as the Brooklyn Bridge of Central Park."

LADIES' PAVILION

Formerly a streetcar shelter, the pavilion was
pushed inside the park by the *Maine* monument

No matter how ordinary, every structure in the park and even those at its edge were
beautifully designed with intricate detail. This ornate pavilion, created as a shelter for
horsecar passengers waiting at the southwest corner of the park, is no exception. It
served that purpose for more than forty years, from its creation in 1871 to 1912, when
it was moved inside the park to make way for the *Maine* monument. It was moved to
the western shore of the lake, where it stands on the Hernshead promontory, near
West Seventy-fifth Street. In the park's early years, a nearby portion of the lake was
reserved in winter for women ice-skaters and called the Ladies' Pond, which may
explain the name for the pavilion.

After long periods of neglect at its location on the lake, the dilapidated pavilion was knocked down by vandals in 1971. The pieces were recovered and reassembled and the structure was firmly anchored with steel rods reaching down into a concrete foundation. The name Hernshead comes from an archaic English pronunciation for "heron." The pavilion overlooks the lake and, while it occasionally provides views of herons and egrets, the site is also popular as a romantic setting for wedding photographs.

PARK VIEW WEST

A publicity shot in Central Park was a must for visiting British bands

Left: In the freewheeling 1960s, a new city administration relaxed the park rules and encouraged "happenings and be-ins" that attracted New York's younger generation. Central Park also became the place to be for the rock stars of this era, if only for publicity photos. The Beatles, the first to arrive, visited the park and enjoyed a luxury suite at the Plaza Hotel. The Dave Clark Five are seen here in 1964, posed against the Central Park West skyline. The Rolling Stones were soon to follow. The San Remo (on the right) and the Majestic (left) are two of the avenue's four twin-towered buildings that went up in the 1930s.

Above: While musical tastes are ever changing, the massive rock in both photos remains an immutable feature of the landscape. Known as Manhattan schist, it is an outcropping of the extremely durable bedrock formed by intense subterranean heat and pressure some 450 million years ago. Underlying all of Central Park and much of Manhattan Island, it provides a strong foundation for New York skyscrapers. The San Remo has had its share of contemporary celebrities. Film director Steven Spielberg and actors Dustin Hoffman and Demi Moore purchased multifloor apartments facing the park, and U2's Bono bought his north tower penthouse from Apple chief Steve Jobs.

THE DAKOTA

One of the grandest apartment blocks of the Gilded Age

Left: People often joked that the Dakota, seen here in stark isolation a few years after it was built in 1884, was as far from the center of civilized New York as the Dakota Territory. The comparison to the remote West was a snide reference to the building's unfashionable West Side location at Seventy-second Street and Eighth Avenue, soon to be renamed Central Park West. But while it faced the park, the building could not compete with the mansions across the park on Fifth Avenue, the undisputed center of society. The Dakota's developer, Singer Sewing Machine executive Edwin Clark, chose the name to stake out a new neighborhood, one with an unmistakably American name and a new future for the aspiring middle class. For people who could not afford a palace, this was an opportunity to live in part of one.

Above: Now framed by more modern buildings, the Dakota is recognized today as the grandest apartment house of the Gilded Age, one that set a new standard of luxury for apartment living. Its wealthy residents include a number of celebrities, of whom the most famous was John Lennon. Well before Lennon's 1980 murder in front of the building, the Dakota had been tinged with an ominous atmosphere portrayed in the 1968 film *Rosemary's Baby*, which told a fictional tale of devilish happenings within the fortresslike building. But the Dakota has overcome all that. It now fulfills its prominent location as a landmark of luxury on the park. Magnolia trees blooming inside the park can be seen on the right.

RIFTSTONE ARCH

A regular haunt for John Lennon and Yoko Ono in the 1970s

Above: When this arch was built in 1862 at the West Seventy-second Street entrance to the park, horseback riders passing through it must have felt as if they were on a ride out in the country. In those days, there were no tall buildings to be seen at the park's edge and the rugged stones of the arch, assembled without mortar, must have appeared like an ancient fixture. By the time of this early twentieth-century photo, the Dakota, with its peaked gable (left), and its neighbor, the Langham, created a more urban setting for the picturesque arch.

Right: On a snowy day a century later, the Riftstone Arch appears just as picturesque as it did in the earlier view. But the Dakota and Langham are now part of a grand boulevard of apartment houses on Central Park West. The tower rising in the center of the photo is the San Remo. John Lennon and Yoko Ono crossed over the arch on their frequent trips from their apartment in the Dakota to stroll through this side of the park. Strawberry Fields, the park area dedicated to Lennon, is nearby.

DANIEL WEBSTER MONUMENT

The great orator's statue still presides over the Seventy-second Street transverse road

Left: Dedicated in 1876 for the nation's centennial, this impressive statue—thirty-four feet high including its base—reflects Daniel Webster's monumental stature in the minds of nineteenth-century Americans. An acclaimed American statesman and orator, he was successful in delaying the Civil War in 1850 shortly before his death in 1852, and after the war was viewed as a symbol of healing. The statue was placed in a prominent spot on the Seventy-second Street transverse road in view of a constant stream of passing carriages.

Above: Today, few people remember the deeds of Daniel Webster (1782–1852), and the oversized statue has likewise lost some of its historic significance. It is not one of the most popular statues in the park. In fact, some critics have likened the stiff figure to a wooden Indian. But it holds its ground as a familiar landmark on the well-traveled Seventy-second Street road where carriages, bike riders, and strollers still pass by.

WEST DRIVE AT SIXTY-SEVENTH STREET

Bringing the automobile to heel with the park's first stoplights

Left: The cars in this 1922 photo have stopped to observe the park's first traffic stoplights, introduced that year at pedestrian crossings. When cars first came on the scene, they were banned from the park, but the Automobile Club of America challenged that ruling in 1899 and won. As more cars entered the park, they clashed with horse carriages and pedestrians and tore up the gravel drives. Park police found it nearly impossible to enforce the eight-miles-per-hour speed limit. In 1912 the Parks Department began asphalting the carriage drives and a few years later the park speed limit was increased to fifteen miles per hour. The age of the automobile had begun. The low building on the left is the sheepfold before its conversion to the Tavern on the Green in the 1930s.

Above: This is the same crossing as in the earlier photo, but the trees now block the view of the Tavern on the Green. Auto traffic is a continuing intrusion into the park and a constant source of debate. Once government officials began to acknowledge the health hazards of auto air pollution in the 1960s, the park was closed to cars on Sundays. Calls for more restrictions, particularly from organized bicycling groups, have made an impact. Currently the park drives are closed to cars on both Saturdays and Sundays and open for limited hours on weekdays. The speed limit is twenty-five miles per hour, not bad considering it was up to fifteen miles per hour nearly a century ago. But the logistics of circumventing traffic around an 843-acre park in the center of Manhattan remain an urban challenge.

COPYRIGHT 1894 BY J S JOHNSTON N.Y.

SHEEP MEADOW

The tradition of Sunday in the park started in the 1890s

Left: Sheep were brought to the meadow in 1870, but people were not always allowed. Early restrictions against walking on the grass and playing sports or conducting other group activities on Sundays discouraged working families whose only day off was on Sunday. The rules were loosened by the 1890s, a time when immigrants accounted for more than half of New York City's population. This group, photographed circa 1894, is playing a game of Copenhagen. The rules of the game have been lost to time, but it was apparently a version of spin the bottle.

Above: In the 1960s, groups were not only allowed but encouraged to assemble on the Sheep Meadow. Parks commissioner Thomas Hoving promoted a series of mass events called Hoving's Happenings. Thousands came to celebrate Halloween, compete in a "Central Park A-Go-Go" dance concert, and watch the 1969 moon landing on huge television screens. People of every cultural and political persuasion also gathered for impromptu "be-ins, love-ins, fat-ins, and gay-ins." But these events and free concerts, including huge turnouts for Barbra Streisand in 1967 and James Taylor in 1979, took their toll on the meadow. It was closed for restoration in 1980 and reopened a year later for quieter activities such as sunbathing and picnicking. The tallest buildings in this southwestern view are the twin towers of the Time Warner Center and, in front of it, the Trump International Hotel and Tower.

SHEEP MEADOW

The first plans for this area of the park designated it as a parade ground

Left: Political rallies were rare in Central Park until the escalating Vietnam War and the growing antiwar movement of the 1960s. Prior to 1966, when the first anti–Vietnam War demonstration assembled on the Mall, the only other political event in Central Park had been a women's suffrage meeting in 1914. Much larger antiwar rallies took place on the Sheep Meadow in 1967 and 1968. The April 27, 1968, rally—seen here against the Upper West Side skyline—was particularly powerful because of the appearance of Coretta Scott King, whose husband, Dr. Martin Luther King Jr., had been assassinated only weeks earlier on April 4. Ironically, the first plans for this area had called for a parade ground for military drills. Olmsted and Vaux strongly objected, even during the years of the Civil War, because they feared it would attract unruly crowds.

Above: After the Sheep Meadow was restored in 1981, large events were relocated to the Great Lawn (and most were later restricted from there as well). At fifteen acres, the meadow is the largest open green space in the park. Even against the backdrop of a modern city, it gives crowded urban dwellers a liberating sense of expansiveness. Ringed by trees, thicker and taller than in Olmsted's day, it restricts the designer's goal of limitless space. But the trees also provide a protective boundary against the city's noise and hard surfaces. A new irrigation system, installed in 2001, maintains the meadow as a lush retreat. It is fenced off from fall to midspring to allow the grass to grow. Once it does, there is no better place to walk barefoot in the city.

TAVERN ON THE GREEN

Manhattan's only restaurant converted from a sheep barn

Above: Larger than it looks in this 1944 photo, the Tavern on the Green was built in 1870 as a sheepfold, housing both the shepherd and the flock of sheep who grazed in the Sheep Meadow. In 1934 Robert Moses sent the sheep to Brooklyn's Prospect Park and converted the building to a restaurant designed to look like an old English inn. Doormen in hunting costumes and cigarette girls in bustles sufficed for an atmosphere of old England. All went well until 1956, when Moses decided to double the restaurant's parking lot by destroying fifty trees in an area frequented by local mothers and children. After Moses rebuffed the women's pleas, they blocked the bulldozer and later won their case in court. The story was on newspaper front pages for days, and was a turning point in Moses's reputation as a park defender.

Right: The restaurant faltered in the 1960s and was jokingly referred to as the "Tavern in the Red." It reopened in 1976 with a decor that was more Vegas than Manhattan. The glass-enclosed dining room is just one of several interior rooms draped with enough crystal chandeliers to light up the park. Encased in thousands of lights, the surrounding trees create a year-round park fantasy. But after three decades of dazzling success as one of the nation's top-grossing restaurants, the Tavern on the Green became the Tavern in the Red again when the operator filed for bankruptcy in September 2009. The Parks Department has since leased the premises to a new operator. Located just inside the park's West Sixty-seventh Street entrance, it still promises to be a glittering tourist attraction.

CAROUSEL

The park has had four carousels, but the latest is over 100 years old

Left: Generations of children have ridden carousels in Central Park, a different carousel in each generation. Seen here in 1945, this was the park's third carousel. The first model in 1871 literally ran on horsepower—a horse and a mule tied to a central pole belowground turned it around. At ten cents a ticket, it cost nearly as much as the average workingman earned in an hour. In 1877 a sympathetic Park Board president cut the fee to five cents. The horse-driven carousel was replaced by a steam-powered version around the turn of the century. That one was destroyed by fire in 1924. The one pictured here suffered the same fate in 1950.

Above: The latest Central Park carousel is the fourth one operating on this site, midpark near West Sixty-fifth Street. While it is the newest replacement, it is a century old. The Parks Department discovered it in storage at an old trolley terminal on Coney Island. A fine example of American folk art, the hand-carved horses have a lot more life than those in the previous version. They were created by master craftsmen Sol Stein and Harry Goldstein of the Artistic Carousel Manufacturing Company of Williamsburg, Brooklyn, in 1908. One of the largest carousels in the United States, its fifty-eight horses and two chariots are ridden by a quarter of a million people each year.

CHILDREN'S PLAYING FIELDS

Maypole dances and celebrations gave way to "boys-only" baseball

Left: Maypole celebrations were popular events for schoolgirls throughout the city's parks in the late nineteenth and early twentieth centuries. This one, photographed in 1912 and sponsored by the Public School Athletic League, was held on a ten-acre meadow in the southwestern corner of the park. Dedicated for open play, it soon became the site for the increasingly popular sport of baseball. While girls danced around the maypole, only boys were allowed to play baseball.

Above: By the 1930s, organized baseball games, still largely played by boys, had squeezed out maypole dances, which moved to other park meadows and eventually disappeared. Robert Moses laid out permanent baseball diamonds here in 1936 and named them the Heckscher Ball Fields after the donor, philanthropist August Heckscher. A multimillion-dollar makeover in 2007 provided improved drainage, irrigation, and playing surfaces. These fields are among the twenty-six ball fields in the park, many of them now used by coed teams. The thirty-team Broadway Show League of cast and stage crew members has played here for more than fifty years.

HECKSCHER PLAYGROUND

Robert Moses led the way in providing playgrounds in the park

Left: When Robert Moses became the city parks commissioner in 1934, Central Park had only one playground. Just three years later it had twenty-two, all equipped with slides, swings, jungle gyms, sandboxes, and benches. This was the first playground, originally created in 1926 with play equipment donated by August Heckscher, and seen here in 1959 with Moses-era swings and benches. The child on the swing is enjoying a wonderful view looking southeast toward the Plaza Hotel on the right and the Sherry-Netherland Hotel on the left.

Above: Carving out New York City playgrounds was one of Robert Moses's lasting achievements. In addition to those in Central Park, he created more than 600 playgrounds throughout the city. Over time, the standard swings and hard play surfaces were considered outdated and were greatly improved. New ideas for more imaginative play were introduced in the 1960s and have steadily expanded with the advent of colorful, safer materials. The three-acre Heckscher Playground, still the largest in Central Park, was completely changed in 2006 into a children's wonderland. Along with new swings, slides, and seesaws, it has a large water feature, a child-size suspension bridge, and a handsome playground building all overlooking the same southeastern view. Although the Plaza Hotel is obscured by trees, the pinnacle of the Sherry-Netherland can still be seen among towering additions.

PINEBANK ARCH

Spanning a bridle path, this cast-iron arch now sees few horses passing underneath

Left: Called an arch, Pinebank is more of a bridge. Its cast-iron span, eighty feet in length, runs between two natural rock outcroppings over the bridle path. Built in 1861, it was spared after two other cast-iron bridges over the bridle path were demolished in the 1930s when the path was shortened. It frames a striking view in this 1942 winter scene looking west toward the twin-towered Century Apartment Building on Central Park West and Sixty-second Street. Built in 1931, the Century is an Art Deco building with machine-age tops and apartments that ranged from one-room flats to eleven-room suites.

Above: The bridge's cast-iron latticework, rusted and missing some handrails and posts, was returned to its full splendor as part of a 1984 restoration. As a final touch, white pines were planted along the right bank. The park's four-mile-long bridle path now has more joggers, dog-walkers, and stroller-pushers than horses—and it's no wonder. In the nineteenth century, horseback riding in the park was a pastime for the wealthy, who often had their own stables nearby. It is still an expensive activity today. Manhattan's last public stable closed in 2007. Horses are now brought down by trailers from a stable in the Bronx—and the park riding rate is $100 per hour. The fence is a temporary protection for fall plantings.

GREYSHOT ARCH

Featuring striking stonework and stylized fleur-de-lis motifs

Above: Even when faced with the pressing need for roads, the park designers ensured that each arch was a thing of beauty. This one, mostly completed by 1860, was well underway at the start of park construction in 1859 in order to support the carriage roads being built along the park's southwestern side. Flanked by buttresses with curved supports and diamond-point posts, the arch has a monumental presence lightened by stylized fleur-de-lis carved into the 100-foot-long balustrade. This photo was taken sometime after 1863, when the balustrade was installed. While the arch was built to support a carriage road, it also provided pathways alongside the road for pedestrians like the ones seen here.

Right: Just as beautiful as when it was built a century and a half ago, the Greyshot Arch is a beckoning passageway from city streets into green surroundings. It is located a short distance inside the park off Central Park West and Sixty-second Street. Although the traffic and noise of Columbus Circle is not far away, the thirty-foot-wide, eighty-foot-long tunnel carries one away from the urban atmosphere. The trees around the arch, noticeably larger than in the older photo, frame the structure's striking stonework.

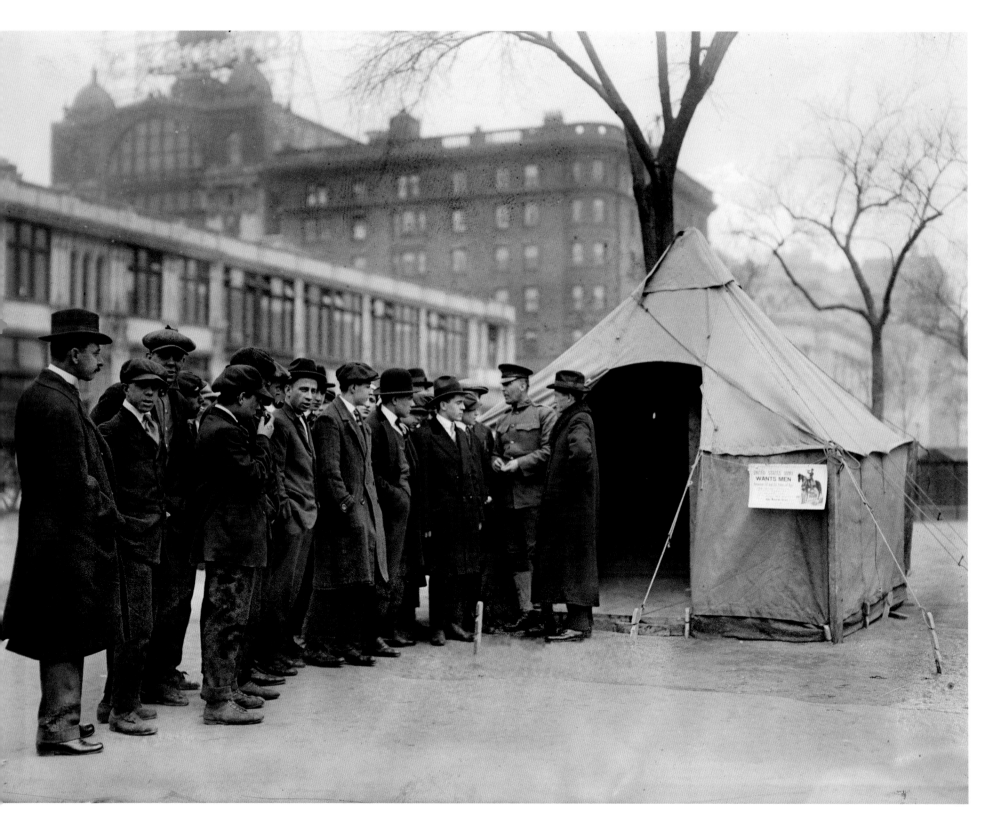

CENTRAL PARK WEST AND SIXTIETH STREET

World War I made an impression on the park's west side

Left: This World War I recruitment center was photographed in 1916 at the southwestern edge of Central Park. With the United States preparing to enter the war in 1917 even parks became centers for recruitment, where able-bodied men between the ages of eighteen and thirty-five could enlist. But it is unlikely that one would have intruded onto Central Park's elegant Fifth Avenue side to the east. Instead of mansions and luxury hotels, commercial buildings lined this corner of the park. Most of the ones seen here were part of a corridor of automobile showrooms.

Above: No longer the cheap side of the park, Central Park West now rivals Fifth Avenue for high-priced living. Glitz and glamour now dominate the southwestern edge of the park. On the left are the Trump International Hotel and Tower, built in 1996, and 15 Central Park West, a residential complex that opened in 2007 as the city's most expensive housing development. Nineteenth-century land values along both sides of the park began to inflate at the start of its construction and continued to rise throughout the twentieth century—and skyrocketed in the twenty-first. The 1.3-acre plot for 15 Central Park West sold for $401 million, making it the most expensive residential site per square foot in Manhattan.

CENTRAL PARK WEST AND FIFTY-NINTH STREET

The Macy's Thanksgiving Day Parade is a New York tradition dating to 1924

Left: The Macy's Thanksgiving Day Parade began in 1924 and was well established as a New York City tradition by the time of this photo in 1941. This is a prime viewing spot along the west side of Central Park. The *Maine* monument at the park's Fifty-ninth Street entrance is on the right. Live animals borrowed from the park zoo were part of the parade in its early years. They were replaced in 1927 by large, animal-shaped balloons, such as this flying fish. The parade was interrupted by World War II from 1942 to 1944 because the rubber used for the balloons was needed for the war effort. The marching bands, floats, and giant balloons started up again in 1945.

Above: The same view today includes only one building shown in the archival photo, the Century Apartments, the white tower in the center background, built in 1931 and saved from demolition by the city's landmark law. In front of it is the new luxury complex 15 Central Park West, which replaced the former Mayflower Hotel, built in 1926 and visible on the far left of the older photo. The glass tower in the foreground is the Trump International Hotel and Tower, built in 1996. Residents and hotel guests in the three buildings, along with those all along Central Park West, enjoy bird's-eye views of the park and the annual Macy's Thanksgiving Day Parade.

COLUMBUS CIRCLE

One of the major points of access to the park

Left: The traffic circle connecting Broadway, Central Park West, Fifty-ninth Street, and Eighth Avenue was a streetcar hub for many years and a major point of access to Central Park. Looking north toward Central Park West, this 1901 photo shows the park on the right and the construction of subway lines under the circle. The subway would make it even easier for working and middle-class people from all over the city to reach the park. The intersection was named Columbus Circle in 1892, the 400th anniversary of Christopher Columbus landing in the New World. Italian Americans, whose numbers were rising rapidly in this period of increasing immigration, dedicated the Columbus monument at the circle's center.

Above: This view was taken from the Time Warner Center, a towering shopping, hotel, and entertainment complex built at Columbus Circle in 2003. It looks west over the newly landscaped Columbus Monument and the park's Fifty-ninth Street entrance. While the subways still run underground, the atmosphere on this side of the park has become quite upscale. The Time Warner Center capitalizes on striking views of the park. Considering the name of the opposite park entrance—Merchants' Gate—the location of the huge commercial complex seems very appropriate today.

MAINE MONUMENT

Of the many monuments to the sunken warship, this is perhaps the grandest of all

Left: Patriotism was on display at the dedication of the *Maine* monument on April 30, 1913, at the Fifty-ninth Street park entrance. The crowd in the red, white, and blue pavilion came to honor the dead who went down on the USS *Maine* in the explosion in Havana Harbor that triggered the Spanish-American War of 1898. Among the ceremony's officials, the most influential was the powerful publisher William Randolph Hearst. His newspaper had provoked the war (the battle cry was "Remember the *Maine*, the Hell with Spain") that gave the United States control of Cuba, Puerto Rico, the Philippines, and Guam. Immediately after the *Maine* went down, he organized a public subscription campaign to build the memorial. While Hearst initially preferred Times Square for the site, he was happy with this location since he owned cheap surrounding land and the grand monument helped raise his property values.

Above: No doubt Olmsted and Vaux would have hated the *Maine* monument. It is reminiscent of the proposed formal entrances to the park that they successfully resisted in the 1860s. The monument is grandiose, to be sure. The figure on top of the pylon is Columbia Triumphant, drawn in a seashell chariot pulled by three sea horses. Cast in bronze recovered from the actual guns of the USS *Maine*, she presides over a collection of other martial figures at the statue's base. But few people today are at all concerned about the nineteenth-century aesthetic battles over monuments in the park, or of the history of the Spanish-American War. Many now believe that the explosion that sank the *Maine* was an accident.

Taken just inside the park's Columbus Circle entrance, this photo of a snowy December day in 1948 looks out on a peaceful urban scene. The entrance is called Merchants' Gate, although no physical gate is in sight here or at any of the other seventeen park entrances named in the 1860s. They are simply passageways through the park's low walls, sometimes marked by pylons with the name of the entrance carved in the stone. Many of the names reflect the nineteenth-century moral value placed on work: scholars, artists, and artisans have gates, along with pioneers, farmers, hunters, miners, woodsmen, mariners, engineers, inventors, and warriors. Women, not credited with any of these occupations in the mid-nineteenth century, also have a gate named in their honor, along with children, saints, and even strangers.

MERCHANTS' GATE

Named in honor of the trade, and not reserved exclusively for their use

The same view on another snowy day now centers on the New Museum of Art and Design, which opened along Columbus Circle in 2008. The museum is a reworking of an earlier building, the Huntington Hartford Museum, which had a controversial history. Hartford, heir to the A&P Grocery fortune, had tried to build a café in the park opposite the Plaza Hotel. Barred from building inside the park, he built his museum at the park's southwestern corner in 1964. From the start, the odd structure, resting on lollipop-shaped columns, drew sharp criticism. Its collection of figurative art was also unpopular in a time when abstract art was all the rage. Vacant for many years, the building was eventually redesigned, but not before a new generation of preservationists tried unsuccessfully to landmark it as an historic structure.

CENTRAL PARK APARTMENTS

One of nineteenth-century New York's most ambitious building projects

This massive apartment block opposite the park was actually eight separate buildings. Each one was named for a Spanish town, hence its nickname of the "Spanish Flats," although many of the large apartments were on double floors. The ambitious development—the largest apartment complex in the city and possibly in the world— was inspired by unlimited views into the park. Built from 1883 to 1885 on Fifty-ninth Street, also known as Central Park South, it took up the entire block between Sixth and Seventh avenues facing the park. It was one of the first and certainly the largest cooperatively owned block of apartment houses. But financing proved difficult for the developer and he was forced to auction the complex. Many who could afford to buy luxury apartments in the 1880s preferred their own homes.

The New York Athletic Club took over this corner of Seventh Avenue and Fifty-ninth Street in 1930 and it has been a stately presence here ever since. Filling out the block where the Central Park Apartments once stood are a series of hotels, also built in the 1930s. In the 1980s, Donald Trump made an unsuccessful attempt to demolish several of the hotels and build a seventy-story apartment tower that would have dwarfed every other building on the street and overshadowed the park. Confronted with strong opposition, he settled for remodeling some of the existing structures and gilding the facades.

RUSTIC SHELTER

The largest rustic wooden structure in the park

Left: Known as Cop Cot—Scottish for "hilltop cottage"—this summerhouse was one of more than a hundred rustic structures in the park. Built in the early 1860s, it was perched on top of a rocky hill near the Sixth Avenue and Central Park South entrance to the park. In the left background are the gables and chimneys of the luxurious Central Park Apartments built in the early 1880s on Central Park South. Rustic shelters were often placed on top of rocky outcroppings and the one in the foreground is typical of these ancient fixtures found throughout the park.

Above: It looks just the same as the original, but this is a replica built in 1985. Like the one in the archival photo, it is also covered with vines, just as Olmsted and Vaux intended, since they preferred park structures that blended in with the landscape. Its hilltop site provides beautiful views of the Pond and the entire southern section of the park. In good weather, local office workers find it a popular spot for lunch breaks. This version of Cop Cot remains the largest rustic wooden structure still standing in the park.

BICYCLING IN THE PARK

Riding in the park could be a liberating experience

Left: The late nineteenth century was the golden age of bicycling, a time when races were held in cities throughout the world and bike riding became a popular activity. It was a liberating experience for women as it was one of that era's few acceptable forms of exercise. Suffragist leader Susan B. Anthony said that bike riding did "more to emancipate women than anything else in the world. It gives them a sense of freedom and self-reliance." The women in this circa-1890 photo felt confident enough to take part in a bicycling parade in Central Park. The one on the right is wearing bicycling "pants," a daring fashion in these days of ankle-length skirts.

Right: Closing the park to cars on Sundays in the 1960s brought in thousands of bike riders. Some are practiced racers, zipping by in streamlined bodysuits and helmets; others, clothes flapping in the breeze and ribbons on their baskets, are out just for the fun of it. Bicycling organizations have been the strongest advocates for keeping cars out of the park and have succeeded in convincing city officials to further limit the days and hours that cars can use the park drives. Thanks to their efforts, Central Park is more parklike today.

CENTRAL PARK AT NIGHT

Nightfall over Central Park brings a unique blend of pastoral and urban beauty

Above: Taken on March 16, 1937, this photo of Central Park's southern end is as much about the city as the park. Central Park has always been seen as a counterpoint to New York City, but over the park's 150-year history, the perspective has changed. In the mid-nineteenth century, the park was envisioned as a pastoral retreat that would blot out its urban surroundings. By 1906, when Charles Ives composed *Central Park in the Dark*, a chamber orchestra piece that created a "picture-in-sounds of nature," the park was still romanticized as an escape from the city. But for the photographer of this scene—as for so many other artists from this era to the present day—the park's most compelling feature is its juxtaposition against the city skyline. The lights of the skyscrapers, including the prominent Essex House built on Central Park South in 1930, sparkle along with the park lights reflected off the snow.

Right: In the 1960s and 1970s, the park endured a period of neglect and lost its romantic image, particularly at night. In 1961 the humorist Ogden Nash wrote: "If you should happen after dark / To find yourself in Central Park, . . . hurry, hurry to the zoo, / And creep into the tiger's lair. / Frankly you'll be safer there." Park crimes have always been highly publicized, but despite a few sensational incidents, the crime rate has remained low—in fact, the lowest of all city precincts. Its reputation as a dangerous place began to change in 1980 with the start of the Central Park Conservancy. While the park is officially closed from 1:00 a.m. to 6:00 a.m., a range of wholesome activities—concerts, family films, and ice-skating—take place at night. As seen from One Central Park West, nightfall over Central Park brings a unique blend of pastoral and urban beauty.

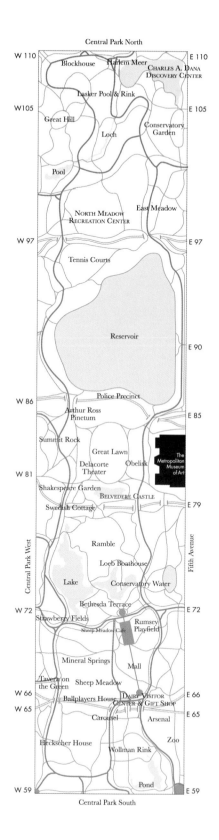